PEGASUS

WORLD'S GREAT PEOPLE

Compiled and Edited by
Manpreet K. Aden

CONTENT

INTRODUCTION

Only a person who has a strong will, a determined mind and a clear perspective looking towards his goal can achieve success. Such a person can even bring about a revolution and rid the society and sometimes even the world of a sickness that had been plaguing it. Over the centuries there have been extraordinary individuals whose ideas, concepts and methods have changed the way we look at things, and often towards other races and cultures. These gifted individuals looked at the differences prevalent in the society and instead of looking towards others, decided that they themselves would initiate to bring about a change in the world. As these individuals set forth to bring about change in our perspectives and that of the world, millions followed them. Some of these individuals took to the centre stage when the world was falling apart and it was mandatory that nations on the whole stayed united.

Including these **Great Persons** in our Pegasus Active Reading is a means to make the young minds aware of their hard work to make the world a friendlier and better place to live together irrespective of our differences. The struggles of these extraordinary individuals remind us of the injustice done towards others and why history should not be repeated.

MAHATMA GANDHI

Mohandas Gandhi is considered the father of the Indian Independence Movement. Through his virtues, simplistic lifestyle and his concept of satyagraha, he led India to its independence. Many civil rights leaders, including Martin Luther King Jr., used Gandhi's concept of non-violent protest as a model for their own struggles.

Early Life of Gandhi

Mohandas Karamchand Gandhi was the last child of his father (Karamchand Gandhi) and his father's fourth wife (Putlibai). As a youth, Gandhi was shy, soft-spoken, and only a mediocre student at school. He was an obedient child though at one point Gandhi experimented with eating meat, smoking, and a small amount of stealing. All this he later regretted.

At 13, Gandhi married Kasturba. They had four sons. Kasturba supported her husband in his endeavours until her death in 1944.

Off to London

In September 1888, aged 18, Gandhi left India without his wife to study law in London. In order to become an English gentleman and fit into the English society, Gandhi spent his first three months in London buying new suits, fine-tuning his English accent, learning French, and taking violin and dance lessons. Three months later, he decided that it all was a waste of time and money and gave them up. He then spent the remainder

Endeavour an attempt to do something difficult or something not done before

of his three-year stay in London being a serious student and living a simple lifestyle.

During this time, Gandhi discovered his life-long passion for vegetarianism. In his search for vegetarian restaurants, Gandhi found and joined the London Vegetarian Society. It was through members of the Society that Gandhi began to really read the **Bhagvad Gita**, a sacred Hindu text. The ideas and concepts he now learned laid the foundations for his later beliefs.

Gandhi successfully passed the bar on June 10, 1891 and sailed back to India. For two years, Gandhi attempted to practice law in India. But he realised that he lacked both knowledge of Indian law and his self-confidence. When he was offered a year-long position to take a case in South Africa, he gladly took it.

Arriving in South Africa

At age 23, leaving his family behind, Gandhi set off for South Africa. He arrived in British-governed Natal in May 1893. It was in South Africa that Gandhi transformed from a very quiet and shy man to a resilient and potent leader against discrimination. The beginning of this transformation occurred during a business trip he soon took after his arrival in South Africa.

Gandhi was to travel from Natal to the capital of the Dutch-governed Transvaal province for his case. When Gandhi boarded the first train of his journey at the Pietermaritzburg station, railroad officials told him to sit in the third-class passenger car. Gandhi, who was holding first-class passenger tickets, refused to move. Then, a policeman forcibly threw him off the train.

Gandhi witnessed several injustices during this trip. As Gandhi talked to other Indians in South Africa (derogatorily called "coolies"), he heard that such incidents were common. It was during this trip that Gandhi decided that he would fight these discriminatory practices until they were stopped.

The Reformer

Gandhi spent the next twenty years working to better Indians' rights in South Africa. In the beginning, he learnt more about Indian grievances,

Resilient *someone who recovers his strength and position quickly*
Discrimination *the act of being partial or treating someone or a group unfairly*

wrote letters to officials, and organized petitions. On May 22, 1894, Gandhi established the Natal Indian Congress (NIC). Soon, Gandhi was the leader of the Indian community in South Africa.

Gandhi with members of the Natal Indian Congress

In 1896, after living three years in South Africa, Gandhi sailed to India to bring his wife and two sons to South Africa. On November 30, 1896, Gandhi and his family headed for South Africa. In his absence, his pamphlet of Indian grievances, known as the **Green Pamphlet**, had been exaggerated and distorted. When Gandhi's ship reached the Durban harbour, it was detained for 23 days. It was because a large, angry mob of whites had assembled at the dock. They believed that Gandhi was returning with two shiploads of Indian passengers to overrun South Africa. When allowed to disembark, Gandhi successfully sent his family off to safety, but he himself was assaulted with bricks, rotten eggs, and fists. Police arrived in time to save Gandhi and escorted him to safety. When Gandhi refused to prosecute those who had assailed him, the violence against him stopped. However, the entire incident strengthened Gandhi's prestige in South Africa.

A Simplified Life

Influenced by the **Gita**, Gandhi wanted to purify his life by following the concepts of **aparigraha** (non-possession) and **samabhava** (equability). Then, getting inspired after reading **Unto This Last** by John Ruskin, Gandhi established a communal living community called Phoenix Settlement just outside of Durban in June 1904. The Settlement was an experiment in communal living, a way to eliminate one's needless possessions and to live in a society with full equality.

In 1906, believing that family life was taking away his full potential as a public advocate, Gandhi took the vow of **brahmacharya** (a vow of abstinence against sexual relations, even with one's own wife). He further restricted his diet. Fasting, he believed, would help still the urges of the flesh.

Satyagraha

After thus refining his life, Gandhi formed his concept of **satyagraha** in late 1906. **Satyagraha** literally means "truth force." Gandhi believed that exploitation was possible only when both the exploited and the exploiter accepted it. But when one saw the universal truth, then one had the power to make change.

In practice, **satyagraha** was a focused and forceful non-violent resistance to a particular injustice. Those who practice **satyagraha** would resist the injustice by refusing to follow an unjust law. While doing so, he would not be angry, would put up with physical assaults, and would not use foul language to smear his opponent.

Satyagraha a policy of noncooperation and opposing a government by using peaceful methods

Gandhi first time used satyagraha in South Africa in 1907 when he organized opposition to the Asiatic Registration Law (known as the Black Act). According to it, all Indians were required to get fingerprinted and to keep registration documents on them at all times. Using **satyagraha**, the Indians refused to do so. Mass protests were organized. After seven years of protest, in June 1914, the Black Act was repealed. Gandhi's method of satyagraha was successful.

Back to India

After staying for twenty long years in South Africa, Gandhi decided to return to India. He sailed to India in January 1915.

Gandhi's struggles and triumphs in South Africa had already reached the Indian shore, so he was treated as a national hero on his return. Gandhi, meanwhile, wanted to start his reforms in India. But a friend advised him that he should first acquaint himself with the people and their troubles.

Gandhi agreed and travelled the country wearing a dhoti and sandals to avoid directing attention to

Reforms to put a stop to ill-practices by introducing better procedures

himself. During this year of observation, Gandhi founded the Sabarmati Ashram in Ahmadabad. Gandhi started living in the ashram with his family.

A year later, Gandhi once again wanted to bring about reforms in India. So, he started to use his influence and preached **satyagraha** to change inequities between Indians. By now his prestige had reached a new high level.

Turning Against the British

As the First World War reached its end, Gandhi started to focus on his fight for Indian self-rule. During the past year, he had observed the pitiable condition of Indian masses and wanted to change it. In 1919, the British gave Gandhi something to fight against - the Rowlatt Act. This Act gave the British in India free-reign to root out "revolutionary" elements and to detain them indefinitely without trial. In response to this Act, Gandhi organized a mass strike, which began on March 30, 1919. Unfortunately, the large scale peaceful protest got out of hand and in many places turned violent.

Mahatma Gandhi with his spinning wheel

The violence that erupted during the protest showed Gandhi that the Indian people did not yet fully understood **satyagraha**. So, Gandhi spent much of the 1920s advocating for **satyagraha** among the Indian masses.

Also during this decade, Gandhi began advocating self-reliance as a way to gain freedom from the British. He advocated that the Indians should spin their own cloth. He popularized this idea by travelling with his own spinning wheel, often spinning yarn while giving a speech.

Participation in Indian Independence Movement

Then, it was Gopal Krishna Gokhale, a leader of the Congress Party, who introduced Mahatma Gandhi to the Indian issues, Indian politics and the Indian people. Then, Gandhi understood the situation perhaps in a better way. Soon after, Gandhi began participating in movements concerning the Indian freedom struggle, prominent among them being his involvement in Champaran and Kheda Satyagraha in 1918-1919.

In Champaran, Bihar, landless serfs, labourers and poor farmers were forced to grow indigo and other cash crops instead of food crops. Suppressed by the ruthless militias of the landlords, they were paid very low prices for them, leaving them in extreme poverty. The villages were kept in extremely unhygienic conditions, and alcoholism, untouchability and purdah were rampant. Now in throes of a devastating famine, the British had levied an oppressive tax which they insisted on increasing in rate.

Untouchability *a practise where higher classes exclude certain lower classes from society*
Purdah *a practice where the women are supposed to keep their face covered so that no men could see them*

Meanwhile, in Kheda, Gujarat, the peasants mostly owned their own lands. However, the district was plagued by poverty, scant resources, alcoholism and untouchability. Moreover, a terrible famine had devastated the area.

The poor peasants were miserable and then the British Government had increased their taxes by 23 percent when the villagers had nothing to eat.

Gandhi's Solution

Hearing about the plight of the farmers, Gandhi proposed satyagraha, non-violence and mass civil disobedience. Though strictly non-violent, Gandhi was proposing real action that the oppressed people readily undertook.

In Champaran, Gandhi established an ashram with the help of his supporters and volunteers. A survey of the village was done to take account of their sufferings. Then, Gandhi started a cleanliness drive in the village, built schools, hospitals and encouraged the villages to give up alcohol and to stop practicing untouchability and purdah.

But his main assault came when he was arrested on the charge of creating unrest. Thousand protested his arrest outside the police station and the court, demanding his release which was done eventually. Gandhi then led organized protests and strike against the landlords, who in the end with the guidance of the British Government, signed an agreement granting more compensation and control over farming to the farmers and cancelled the revenue hike until the famine ended. After this revolt, people began addressing him as **Bapu** (Father) and **Mahatma** (Great Soul).

In Gujarat, Gandhi's chief lieutenant, Sardar Vallabhbhai Patel along with a few other Gandhians, gave the villagers direction in their struggle. They helped the villagers to organize a major tax revolt. The peasants of Kheda signed a petition demanded the tax for that year scrapped due to famine. The petition was rejected and the villagers were threatened to pay the tax or lose their property as well along with arrest.

The tax withheld, and the government sent thugs to seize the farmer's property. The farmers did not resist arrest, nor retaliate to the force employed. The revolt was astounding in terms of discipline and unity. The famers in Kheda remained united in spite of the situation. The government finally made an honourable agreement. The tax for the year in question, and the next was suspended, the increased rate was reduced and all confiscated property was returned. Gandhi's method of satyagraha spread like wildfire throughout the country and he became a defining figure in Indian politics.

The Non-Cooperation Movement

The Non-Cooperation Movement under the leadership of Gandhi and the Indian National Congress went underway from September 1920 to February 1922. It was a new awakening in the Indian Independence Movement. After a series of events including the Jallianwala Bagh Massacre, Gandhi realized that they would never get anything fairly from the British. So, he withdrew the nation's co-operation from the British Government and launched the Non-Cooperation Movement. Millions of Indians encouraged the movement.

Confiscate to seize or take control of someone's property as punishment

This movement though failed but it shook the British authorities.

Civil Disobedience Movement

In December 1929, Mahatma Gandhi led the Civil Disobedience Movement which was launched in the Congress Session. The aim of this movement was a complete disobedience of the orders of the British Government. During the movement it was decided that India would celebrate January 26 as its Independence Day. On January 26, 1930, meetings were held all over the country and the Congress tricolour was hoisted. The British Government tried to restrain the movement and resorted to brutal firing, killing hundreds of people. Thousands were arrested along with Gandhi and Jawaharlal Nehru. But the movement had spread across the country. Following this, Round Table Conferences were arranged by the British and Gandhi attended the second Round Table Conference at London. But the conference was a failure and the movement revived.

Dandi March

However, a momentous event-Dandi salt march-changed the course of the Indian struggle for freedom. It was launched under the unparalleled leadership of M. K. Gandhi. With this historic event, the Civil Disobedience Movement was formally introduced on a nation-wide basis and all segments of the Indian community plunged into it.

Circumstances Leading to the Dandi March

The first step to initiate nationwide Civil Disobedience was the Dandi March.

According to the British salt tax law, the sale or manufacture of salt by any other source barring the British Government would be a criminal offense, liable for punishment by law. The low-lying coastal regions of the country had extensive reserves of salt, easily available to the labourers. The new salt tax law, however, forced them to buy salt instead of collecting it for free. This one cause united the country like never before.

The Commencement of the Dandi March

Gandhi pleaded with the Viceroy to review the law but the Viceroy turned a deaf ear to Gandhi's pleas. In his letter to Lord Irwin, Gandhi wrote; "If my letter makes no appeal to your heart, on the eleventh day of his month I shall proceed with such co-workers of the Ashram as I can take, to disregard the provision of the Salt Laws." Then, as no reform took place, Gandhi embarked on his 321.87 km long Dandi March on March 12. Gandhi's entourage consisted of seventy nine members of Sabarmati Ashram.

Gandhi during the Dandi March

Viceroy a person sent to rule a colony by a king and queen

In his journey to Dandi, Gandhi's trail increased in size as thousands of inspired followers joined him in his march. On March 6, Gandhi, on Dandi beach, breached the British salt laws. He picked up a fistful of salt and mud and made salt by boiling it in seawater. His followers followed his example and made salt. It was decided that the crusade against the salt tax would be carried on till April 13th.

Thus began a momentous, national endeavour among Indians to make salt. Thousands thronged the beaches to collect loose salt. Indian-made salt was soon sold across the country. Peaceful picketing and marches were also conducted. The British responded to the movement with mass arrests.

When Gandhi announced that he planned a march on the government-owned Dharasana Saltworks, the British arrested Gandhi and imprisoned him without trial. But the arrest had little effect on the awakened masses. Poet Mrs. Sarojini Naidu took over the movement and led 2,500 marchers to the saltworks. The marchers were beaten with

Breach something being broken; inability to do something which should have been done my law.

clubs on their heads and shoulders by the awaiting British soldiers. The international press watched as the marchers did not even raise their hands to defend themselves. The news of the brutal beating of peaceful protesters shocked the world.

To prevent further humiliation, British Viceroy Lord Irwin met Gandhi. The two men agreed on the Delhi Pact, which granted limited salt production and set free all the peaceful protestors in jail as long as Gandhi called off the protests.

Quit India Movement

The Quit India Movement was the final step towards India's independence under the leadership of Mahatma Gandhi.

In 1939, with the outbreak of war between Germany and Britain, India was announced to be a party to the war as it was part of the British Empire. The Congress Working Committee, however, objected to India being led into a war it was not part of. Responding to this declaration, the Viceroy issued a statement on October 17 where he claimed that Britain is waging a war to strengthen peace in the world. He also stated that after the war, the government would initiate modifications in the Act of 1935, in accordance to the desires of the Indians.

Gandhi's reaction to this statement was; 'the old policy of divide and rule is to continue. The Congress has asked for bread and it has got stone.' Meanwhile, in England Chamberlain was succeeded by Churchill as the Prime Minister and the Conservatives, who assumed power in England, gave no heed to Indian demands. In order to pacify the Indians in the circumstance of worsening war situation, the Conservatives were forced to concede some demands of the Indians. But both the Congress and Muslim League rejected the offer.

In this atmosphere of dissatisfaction, Gandhi met the Congress Working Committee in Wardha and revealed his plan to launch Individual Civil Disobedience. Once again, satyagraha became a powerful weapon to wage a war against the British. It was widely used as a mark of protest against the unwavering stance assumed by the British. Anti war speeches ricocheted in all corners of the country, urging people not to support the government in its war endeavours. Almost 14,000 satyagrahi's were

Ricocheted *the rebounding of something after it has struck a surface*

arrested. On December 3, 1941, the Viceroy ordered the acquittal of all the satyagrahis. However, as the situation in Europe intensified, the movement was withdrawn.

Protestors during the Quit India Movement

Gandhi's call for Quit India

Soon, however, Gandhi announced 'Quit India' as the war cry. Gandhi realized that time was ripe to take some strong and quick actions. He wrote a series of articles in **Harijan** where he urged the people to rise in action. To give effect to the Mahatma's views, The Congress Working Committee adopted the 'Quit India' Resolution, on

Acquittal *an act of discharge given by a court stating that the convicted person is not guilty*

July 14, 1942. The All India Congress Committee accepted this resolution with some modifications, on August 8, 1942 in Bombay.

Immediately, on August 9, Mahatma Gandhi, Vallabhbhai Patel, Jawaharlal Nehru and Abul Kalam Azad were arrested. Gandhi's 'do or die' call for the people created an upheaval in the country. At the same time, Gandhi mentioned specifically that mass movement should be conducted following non violent means. Viceroy Lord Linlithgow, adopted a policy of harsh repression all over the country and gory instances of British atrocities abounded all over. Unlike other movements, Quit India Movement captured the quintessence of a 'spontaneous' rising by the people.

The Quit India Movement, meanwhile, unfolded in four phases. In its first phase there were strikes, demonstrations and processions. This phase lasted for three to four days. The factory and mill workers rose to the cause and displayed maximum vigour and enthusiasm.

Raids of municipal and government buildings characterized the second phase of the movement.

Quintessence it is the most perfect picture or description of something
Atrocities a brutal and violent act done especially in a war

Police stations, post offices and railway stations were attacked and set ablaze. Attempts were made by the agitated mobs to capture court buildings. Troops fired to control mob fury. September 1942 marked the beginning of the movement's third phase. With the emergence of the movement into the fourth phase, it gained back its peaceful character and extended till Mahatma Gandhi was released from prison in May, 1944.

Quit India movement was Gandhi's final bid to secure India's independence. Although, many diverse political ideologies were in the Indian National Movement at that time, yet it was Gandhi's satyagraha that strongly challenged the British authorities. India was at the very threshold of Independence by the end of Quit India movement.

Gandhi and Partition of India

When Gandhi was released from prison in 1944, unfortunately, huge disagreements between Hindus and Muslims had arisen. The Muslims feared they would have no political influence if they stayed in India. Thus, they wanted six provinces in northwest India to become an independent country. Gandhi opposed partition of India.

Gandhi was unable to bridge their differences. Massive violence erupted.

The British, witnessing what seemed sure to become a violent civil war, decided to leave India in August 1947. Before leaving, the British persuaded the Hindus, against Gandhi's wishes, to agree to a partition plan. On August 15, 1947, Great Britain granted India independence and also to the newly formed Muslim country of Pakistan. Violence between the Hindus and Muslims reached unprecedented levels as the Hindus marched across to India and the Muslims went to Pakistan.

To stop this widespread violence, Gandhi once again went on a fast. The fast began on January 13, 1948. Realizing that the frail and aged Gandhi could not withstand a long fast, both sides worked together to create peace.

Assassination

Unfortunately, there were a few radical Hindu groups who believed that Gandhi was responsible

Civil War *a war between two political factions within a country*

for the partition. On January 30, 1948, the 78-year-old Gandhi spent his last day as he had many others. A few minutes past 5 p.m., when it was time for the prayer meeting, Gandhi began the walk to Birla House supported by his grandnieces. A crowd had surrounded him as he walked. Then, a young Hindu named Nathuram Godse stopped before him and bowed. Gandhi bowed back. Immediately, Godse rushed forward and shot Gandhi three times. Although Gandhi had survived five other assassination attempts, this time, Gandhi fell to the ground, dead.

Mahatma Gandhi assassinated

Philosophy of Mahatma Gandhi

The evolution of Mohandas Karamchand Gandhi into the 'Mahatma' hinges on the principles that were the guiding light of his life. Till his last breath, he unflinchingly adhered to these philosophies now called 'Gandhism'.

Truth

Truth or 'Satya' was the sovereign principle of Mahatma Gandhi's life. His life was an eternal conquest to discover truth. Gandhi maintained that the concept of truth is above and beyond all other considerations and one must unfailingly embrace truth throughout one's life.

Satyagraha

Gandhiji pioneered the term satyagraha which literally translates to 'an endeavour for truth.' In the context of Indian freedom movement, Satyagraha meant the resistance to the British oppression through mass civil obedience. Truth or Satya and nonviolence were pivotal to the Satyagraha movement and Gandhi ensured that the millions of Indians seeking an end to British rule adhere to these basic principles steadfastly.

Non-violence

The principle of non-violence or Ahimsa has been integral to many Indian religions and Mahatma Gandhi espoused for total non-violence in the Satyagraha movement to seek India's freedom.

Khadi

Khadi, a hand spun and hand-woven cloth embodies the simplicity synonymous with Gandhi's persona. Gandhi embraced the practice of weaving his own clothes from the thread he himself spun and encouraged others to follow suit. Khadi was used as a tool against the British industrial might and to create rural employment in India.

Literary Works

Besides being the greatest leader of 20th century, Mahatma Gandhi was a good writer and authored several books. He was the editor of a newspaper called **Harijan** in Gujarati, Hindi and English,

Indian Opinion while in South Africa and, **Young India**, in English, and **Navajivan**, a Gujarati monthly, on his return to India. Gandhi also wrote his autobiography, **My Experiments with Truth**, **Satyagraha in South Africa** about his struggle there, **Hind Swaraj or Indian Home Rule**, a political pamphlet, and a paraphrase in Gujarati of **John Ruskin's Unto This Last**. He also wrote extensively on vegetarianism, diet and health, rural reforms, **Gita**, religion, social reforms, etc.

ABRAHAM LINCOLN

Abraham Lincoln was the sixteenth President of the United States. He led the country to victory during the American Civil War and contributed profoundly towards ending in America. The former president is also credited with establishing a 'Republican form of government' in America. Ranked among the greatest US presidents, he was assassinated in 1865.

Early Life

Born on February 12, 1809, in a log cabin in backwoods Hardin County, Kentucky, Lincoln grew up on newly broken pioneer farms of the frontier. His father, Thomas Lincoln, was a migratory carpenter and farmer. Little is known of his mother, Nancy Hanks, who died in 1818, soon after the family settled in the wilds of what is now Spencer County, Indiana. Thomas Lincoln soon married Sarah Bush Johnston, a widow. She was a kind and affectionate mother to Abraham. Abraham had almost no formal schooling but he taught himself, repeatedly reading a small stack of books. His first glimpse of the wider world came in a voyage downriver to New Orleans on a flatboat in 1828. In 1830, the Lincolns moved to Macon County, Illinois.

In 1831, the young Lincoln settled in the village of New Salem. There he began working in a store and managing a mill. His sincerity and capability won respect that was strengthened by his ability to hold his own in the roughest society. Later in New Salem, Lincoln was a partner in a grocery store; he

County it is a small administrative district of a country also became a surveyor, was village postmaster, and did various odd jobs, including rail splitting. All the while, he improved his education and studied law.

Early Political Career

In 1834, Lincoln was elected to the state legislature, in which he served four successive terms. In 1836 he obtained his license as an attorney, and the next year he moved to Springfield, where he became a law partner of John T. Stuart. His practice steadily increased. More partnerships followed with Stephen T. Logan and William H. Herndon. Lincoln displayed great ability in law, a ready grasp of argument, sincerity and lucidity of speech.

In 1842, he married Mary Todd after a troubled courtship. Continuing his interest in politics, he served one term in Congress (1847–49). He remained obscure, however, and his attacks as a Whig on the motives behind the Mexican War seemed unpatriotic to his constituents, so he lost popularity at home. Lincoln worked hard for the election of the Whig candidate, Zachary Taylor, in 1848, but when he was not rewarded with the

Lucidity something said which is easy to understand

office he desired, he decided to retire from politics and return to practicing law.

Prairie Lawyer

In the early 1800s, as there were not many law schools, most lawyers preferred learning law through hands-on experience rather than in a classroom. Many were taken on as apprentices by experienced practitioners who taught them firsthand how to effectively argue a case. Lincoln, however, taught himself law without an apprenticeship, memorizing Blackstone's **Commentaries on the Laws of England**. He also learned by heart '**Greenleaf on evidence**, Chitty's **Pleadings**, and Story's **Equity**,' rehearsing cases aloud, analyzing some legal point from various angles until he understood the essence of the problem.

After studying on his own, Lincoln became registered by the Sangamon County Court. He then took his bar exam—an oral questioning by practicing attorneys on the history and technical nuances of the law. Lincoln answered the questions without a fault. He received his license and immediately took on cases.

Apprentice a young person who works for someone in order to learn a trade

Lincoln in a law office

At that time, not all counties had full time judges. Therefore, a system was adopted whereby state supreme court justices would complete a circuit of local county seats twice a year to hear cases. Lawyers such as Lincoln could earn money by travelling with the justices to settle local disputes. As a lawyer, Lincoln earned part of his income by travelling in this manner between 1843 and 1853 doing his most effective legal work. In the supreme court of Illinois, he won nearly all of the 243 cases he argued. This earned him a reputation as a lawyer's lawyer who was always prepared. Lincoln also gained a reputation for his honesty. 'Resolve to be honest at all events,' he advised young attorneys, 'and if in your own judgment you cannot be an honest lawyer, resolve to be honest without being a lawyer'.

1851

By the mid 1850s, Lincoln's cases focused largely on the competing transportation interests of river barges and railroads. In one prominent 1851 case, he represented the Alton & Sangamon Railroad in a dispute with a shareholder, James A. Barret. Barret had refused to pay the balance promised to the railroad on the grounds that it had changed its originally planned route. Lincoln argued that as a matter of law a corporation is not bound by its original charter when that charter can be amended in the public interest, that the newer route proposed by Alton & Sangamon was superior and less expensive, and that accordingly, the corporation had a right to sue Barret for his delinquent payment. Lincoln won this case, and this case was cited by several other courts throughout the United States.

Charter *a document issued by the government where the rights of a particular group are clearly written*

Lincoln was involved in more than 5,100 cases in Illinois alone during his 23-year legal practice. Lincoln and his partners appeared before the Illinois Supreme Court more than 400 times.

The Election of 1860 Brings Abraham Lincoln to the White House

The central issue of the presidential election of 1860 was slavery. Battles over the spread of slavery to new states had gripped the United States throughout the 1850s, and were intensified by the Kansas-Nebraska Act of 1854.

Following the passage of this Act, Abraham Lincoln, who had given up on politics after one unhappy term in Congress, returned to the political arena. In Illinois, he began attacking the legislation and particularly, Senator Stephen A. Douglas. When Douglas ran for re-election in 1858, Lincoln opposed him. Douglas won that election, but the seven Lincoln-Douglas Debates they held across Illinois were mentioned in newspapers around the country, raising Lincoln's political profile.

Slavery a practice of keeping other human beings as slaves and forcing them to work for their owner

Legislation a new law or a set of laws passed by the government

In late 1859, Lincoln was invited to give a speech at Cooper Union in Manhattan. He crafted a speech denouncing slavery and its spread. The speech was a triumph and made Lincoln an overnight political star in New York City.

Lincoln Recovers from his Defeat

In 1859, Lincoln reassessed his political future. He, apart from his busy law practice, started giving speeches outside of Illinois, in Wisconsin, Indiana, Ohio, and Iowa. He also spoke in Kansas, which had been the place of bitter violence between pro-slavery and anti-slavery forces in the 1850s.

All Lincoln's speeches focused on the issue of slavery. He denounced it as an evil institution, and spoke out forcefully against it spreading into new areas. He also criticized Stephen Douglas, who had been promoting the concept of 'popular sovereignty,' in which citizens of new states could vote on whether or not to accept slavery. Lincoln denounced popular sovereignty as a 'stupendous humbug.'

An Invitation to Speak in New York City

In October 1859, Lincoln was at home in Springfield, Illinois, when he received, by telegram, another invitation to speak. It was from a Republican Party group in New York City. The address in New York was to take place on February 27, 1860. Lincoln put considerable time and effort into crafting the address he was to deliver in New York.

An Iconic Image is Snapped by Matthew Brady

In February, Lincoln had to take five separate trains over the course of three days to reach New York City. On the day of the speech, Lincoln took a stroll on Broadway with some men from the Republican group who were hosting his speech. At the corner of Bleecker Street, Lincoln visited the studio of famed photographer Matthew Brady, and had his portrait taken.

The image, also known as "Cooper Union Portrait" became iconic, and would later be the basis for campaign posters during the 1860 election.

The Cooper Union Address

As Lincoln took the stage that evening at Cooper Union, he faced an audience of 1,500 spectators. Most of them were Republicans, and among them were such luminaries as the editor of the antislavery **New York Tribune**, Horace Greeley. Lincoln's address was extremely effective and it surpassed all expectations.

Lincoln was able to show that the founding fathers had intended Congress to regulate slavery. He named the men who had signed the Constitution and who had later voted, while in Congress, to regulate slavery. He also demonstrated that George Washington himself, as President, had signed a bill into law that regulated slavery.

Newspapers carried his speech the next day. The publicity he got was astounding, and Lincoln went on to speak in several other cities in the east before returning to Illinois. That summer the Republican Party held its nominating convention in Chicago. Abraham Lincoln received the party's nomination above a few others.

Lincoln Seeks the Republican Nomination

Lincoln's ambition to become undisputed leader of the Republicans in Illinois began to evolve into a desire to run for the Republican nomination for president. The first step was to gain the support of the Illinois delegation at the state Republican convention in Decatur in early May 1860.

Lincoln supporters talked to his relatives and located a fence Lincoln had helped build 30 years earlier. Two rails from the fence were painted with pro-Lincoln slogans and were carried into the Republican state convention. Lincoln, who was known by the nickname "Honest Abe," was now called the "rail candidate." He grudgingly accepted the new nickname of "The Rail Splitter."

Lincoln's Success at the Chicago Convention

The Republican Party held its 1860 convention later that May in Chicago. Lincoln himself did not attend it. At the convention, William Seward, a senator from New York, was the favourite for the nomination. Seward was ardently anti-slavery,

Grudgingly *showing unwillingness to do something*

and had a higher national profile than Lincoln. However, Lincoln won the nomination.

Back home in Springfield, Lincoln visited the office of a local newspaper on May 18 and received the news of his nomination by telegraph. He walked home to tell his wife Mary that he was the Republican nominee for president.

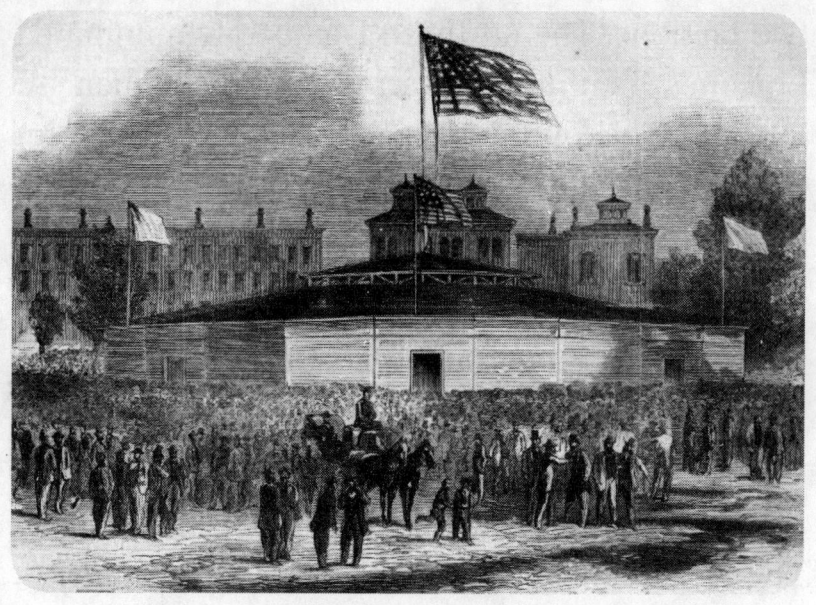

Lincoln nominated at Chicago Convention

The 1860 Presidential Campaign

Lincoln had little to do in the time between nomination and elections in November. Members of their party held rallies and torchlight parades. A number of other prominent Republicans travelled the country campaigning for Lincoln and his running mate, Hannibal Hamlin, a Republican senator from Maine.

Rival Candidates in 1860

In the 1860 election, the Democratic Party split into two factions. The northern Democrats nominated Lincoln's perennial rival, Senator Stephen A. Douglas. The southern Democrats nominated John C. Breckenridge, the incumbent vice president, a pro-slavery man from Kentucky.

Those who felt they could support neither party formed the Constitutional Union Party and nominated John Bell of Tennessee.

The Election of 1860

The presidential election was held on November 6, 1860. Lincoln did very well in the northern states, and he won a landslide victory in the Electoral College. Even if the Democratic Party had not split, it is likely that he still would have won the election.

The 1860 election was crucial as it came at a time of national crisis and it brought Abraham Lincoln to the White House. The train that brought him to Washington was heavily guarded as rumours of his assassination attempts were rampant.

The issue of separation of the southern states was being talked about even before the 1860 election, and Lincoln's election intensified the move in the South to split with the Union. When Lincoln was inaugurated on March 4, 1861, it became certain that the nation was on an inescapable path towards war. Indeed, the American Civil War began the next month.

The American Civil War and Abraham Lincoln

After Abraham Lincoln became the President of the United States, the southern states, of which Lincoln only won 2 of 996 counties, began quickly withdrawing from the Union and forming their own nation, the Confederate States of America. Abraham Lincoln and the majority in the north would not allow this to happen. As a result, an American Civil War was imminent. The war was greatly feared but also fiercely anticipated by both the sides.

Troops during the American Civil War

In April 1861, the Confederates fired on South Carolina's Fort Sumter and the fort was forced to surrender under heavy fire. Abraham Lincoln called for 75,000 volunteers to recapture Union forts and quell the uprising. Four more southern states, including Virginia, withdrew from the Union and the American Civil War had started.

Militarily, the north was on the verge of losing the war until the battle of Antietam. It was the single bloodiest day in American history. Though victory was still nowhere in sight for the north, Abraham Lincoln now at least had enough political influence to put into law the Emancipation Proclamation. The proclamation freed liberated slaves in southern states. The Proclamation not only had political motivations but it also helped to weaken the southern economy as freed black slaves were now allowed to join the ranks of the Union army. By the end of the war about 179,000 black men served in the army and about 19,000 served in the navy.

Lincoln had always faced the northern opposition to war but none so drastically until after the battle of Gettysburg. While Gettysburg was a great northern victory, Lincoln had to initiate the war's second draft to replace the staggering 23,000 Union casualties. The northern citizens weren't happy and violence too took place. The most notable example is the New York City Draft Riots. The riots were put down and Lincoln delivered his famous Gettysburg address.

Gettysburg proved to be the turning point in the American Civil War. The confident north was now led by General Ulysses S. Grant army commander. Meanwhile war continued and despite the Republican fears, Lincoln won the presidential

Riot a violent disorder caused by a group of people
Emancipation to free someone or a group from social, political and legal restrictions

elections of 1864, defeating his democrat opponent George B. McClellan.

The devastating American Civil War came to a end on April 9, 1865 when General Robert E. Lee surrendered to General Ulysses S. Grant at Appomattox Court House in Virginia. Lincoln could now focus on rebuilding the relations between the north and the south. When asked how defeated Confederates should be treated, Lincoln responded 'Let 'em up easy'.

What is the Emancipation Proclamation?

The Emancipation Proclamation consisted of two executive orders issued by U.S. President Abraham Lincoln during the Civil War. The orders did not end slavery, which happened on December 18, 1865 with the passage of the 13th Amendment to the Constitution.

Lincoln issued the first order on September 22, 1862, however, which stated that if the rebels did not end the Civil War and rejoin the Union by January 1, 1863, then all slaves in the Confederacy would be free.

Lincoln issued the second order on, January 1, 1863, as the nation entered its third year of a bloody and expensive Civil War. According to the second order, all slaves in the seceded states were free. This proclamation named the specific states to which the order applied.

Though no single slave was freed due to the proclamation, it changed the character of the war from a war fought to preserve the Union into a war for freedom.

Abraham Lincoln and the Gettysburg Address

Abraham Lincoln's Gettysburg Address is one of the most quoted speeches in American history. Though the speech was short but it was heartfelt and was delivered at the precise time when the nation was engulfed in crisis.

The Battle of Gettysburg had taken place in rural Pennsylvania for three days in July 1863. Thousands of men had died both on the Union and Confederate sides. The magnitude of the battle had stunned the nation. Lincoln was meanwhile very concerned and wanted to make a public statement explaining why it is necessary to keep on fighting the war. The moment he was waiting for came in November.

A large number of union soldiers had died at Gettysburg. They had been hastily buried but now months later, they were going to be properly buried. A ceremony was to be held to dedicate the new cemetery and Lincoln was invited to offer his remarks.

Lincoln during his Gettysburg Address

The program that day began with a procession from the town of Gettysburg to the site of the new cemetery. As Lincoln rose to give his address, the crowd listened intently. Some accounts describe the crowd applauding at points in the speech. The brevity of the speech may have surprised some, but it seems that those who heard the speech realized they had witnessed something important.

Significance of the Gettysburg Address

In the famous opening words, 'Four score and seven years ago,' Lincoln does not refer to the US Constitution, but to the Declaration of Independence. That is important as Lincoln was invoking Jefferson's phrase that 'all men are created equal' which was central to the American Government.

In Lincoln's view, the Constitution was an imperfect document which was always evolving. And it had, in its original form, legalized slavery. By invoking the Declaration of Independence, Lincoln was able to make his argument about equality, and the purpose of the Civil War being a 'new birth of freedom.'

Lincoln's lines at the conclusion, that 'government of the people, by the people, and for the people, shall not perish from the earth' has been extensively quoted and cited as the essence of the American system of government.

1864 Re-election

The 'Emancipation Proclamation' came into effect on January 1, 1863. With this, abolition of slavery in rebel states became a national goal. However, Lincoln did not stop there; he went ahead to devote himself to the passage of the thirteenth amendment to abolish slavery permanently throughout the nation. Based on this agenda, Lincoln was once again elected as the president. He delivered his second inaugural speech on March 4, 1965. At that time, slavery was dead and the rebels were no more a threat.

Reconstruction and preparations to reintegrate the southern states and what to do with Confederate leaders and the freed slaves soon started. Determined to find a course that would reunite the nation again, Lincoln urged that speedy elections under generous terms be held throughout the war

Abolition *to put an end to a law or system*
Reconstruction *a process where something is changed or improved*

in southern areas. His Amnesty Proclamation of December 8, 1863, offered pardons to those who had not held a Confederate civil office, had not mistreated Union prisoners, and would sign an oath of allegiance.

Critical decisions had to be made as southern states were subdued. Slowly and gradually the southern states were made part of the union. The Radicals, however, thought that he was too lenient on the rebels.

Lincoln also visited Richmond after it was taken by the Union forces and to make a public gesture of sitting at Jefferson Davis' own desk, symbolically saying to the nation that the President of the United States held authority over the entire land. He was greeted at Richmond as a conquering hero by freed slaves, whose sentiments were epitomized by one admirer's quote, 'I know I am free for I have seen the face of Father Abraham and have felt him.'

Redefining Republicanism

Lincoln's rhetoric defined the issues of the war for the nation, the world, and posterity. The Gettysburg

Rhetoric an effective manner of using language in order to influence others

Address defied Lincoln's own prediction that 'the world will little note, nor long remember what we say here.' As early as the 1850s, a time when most political rhetoric focused on the sanctity of the Constitution, Lincoln shifted emphasis to the Declaration of Independence as the foundation of American political values.

The Declaration's emphasis was on freedom and equality for all irrespective of their caste, colour or race, and not on the Constitution's tolerance of slavers. His position gained strength because he highlighted the moral basis of republicanism. In his Gettysburg Address Lincoln redefined the American nation, arguing that it was born not in 1789 but in 1776, 'conceived in Liberty, and dedicated to the proposition that all men are created equal.' By emphasizing the importance of equality, he rejected the claims of the state sovereignty.

Domestic Measures

As president, Lincoln exercised his veto power only four times. He signed the Homestead Act in 1862, making millions of acres of government-held land in the West available for purchase at very low cost. The Morrill Land-Grant Colleges Act, also signed in 1862, provided government grants for state agricultural colleges in each state. The Pacific Railways Acts of 1862 and 1864 granted federal support for the construction of the United States' First Transcontinental Railroad.

Other important legislation passed under the leadership of Lincoln were two measures to raise revenues for the Federal government: tariffs (a policy with long precedent), and a Federal income tax (which was new).

Lincoln also presided over the expansion of the federal government's economic influence in several other areas. The creation of the system of national banks by the National Banking Acts of 1863, 1864 and 1865 allowed the creation of a strong national financial system. The Legal Tender Act of 1862 established the United States Currency Note. It was the first paper currency in the United States issued during the revolution to increase money supply to pay for fighting the war.

Assassination

Originally, John Wilkes Booth, a well-known actor and a Confederate spy, had decided to kidnap Lincoln and free him in exchange of release of Confederate prisoners. But after attending an April 11 speech in which Lincoln promoted voting rights for blacks, Booth changed his plans.

He learnt that the President and First Lady would be attending Ford's Theatre. Without his main bodyguard Ward Hill Lamon, Lincoln left to attend the play 'Our American Cousin' on April 14, 1865.

Lincoln's assassination

As a lone bodyguard wandered, and Lincoln sat in his state box in the balcony, Booth crept up behind the President and waited for what he thought would be the funniest line of the play ('You sock-dologizing old man-trap'), hoping the laughter would muffle the gunshot. Just as the laughter began, Booth jumped into the box and fired from his revolver at point blank range aiming at Lincoln's head. Major Henry Rathbone momentarily grappled with Booth but was cut by Booth's knife. Booth then leaped to the stage and shouted 'Sic semper tyrannis!' (Thus always to tyrants). He escaped despite a broken leg. 12 days later, he was caught in a Virginia barn house and shot.

Religious and Philosophical Beliefs

In March 1860, in a speech in New Haven, Connecticut, Lincoln said regarding slavery, 'Whenever this question shall be settled, it must be settled on some philosophical basis. No policy that does not rest upon some philosophical public opinion can be permanently maintained.'

There were few people who strongly or directly influenced Lincoln's moral and intellectual development and perspectives. Lacking a formal education, Lincoln's personal philosophy was shaped by 'an amazingly retentive memory and a passion for reading and learning.' Even as a child, Lincoln largely rejected organized religion, but throughout his life he believed in the Calvinistic 'doctrine of necessity'. As Lincoln matured, and especially during his term as president, the idea of a divine will somehow interacting with human affairs increasingly influenced his public expressions.

In claiming that all men were created free, Lincoln and the Whigs argued that this freedom required economic advancement, expanded education, territory to grow, and the ability of the nation to absorb the growing immigrant population.

It was the 'Declaration of Independence' that Lincoln most relied on to oppose any further territorial expansion of slavery.

NELSON MANDELA

Nelson Mandela was the most significant black leader who stood against racism and apartheid (a rigid policy that separates nonwhites from whites) in South Africa, while many in the world were silent. He dreamt of a democratic and free society in which people live together in harmony with equal opportunities. His words, 'the struggle is my life', show his determination to fight against apartheid and racism in South Africa, the goal he had set almost four decades back. He succeeded in imparting equality and justice to his people for which he received the Nobel Peace Prize in 1993.

Early Life

Nelson Mandela was born Rolihlahla on July 18, 1918 in the small village of Mvezo to a chief named Gadla Henry Mphakanyiswa. While Mandela was still an infant, the colonial authorities deprived Mandela's father of his chief status and he moved his family to Qunu. Mphakanyiswa played an important role in Dalindyebo's ascension in whose house Mandela stayed, to the Thembu throne. Since childhood Mandela lived in a family with rich cultural heritage and amid royalty. He was the first in his family to attend school. It was in school that the young Rolihlahla was given the name Nelson.

Mandela's father died when he was nine years old. He came under the guardianship of regent Jongintaba. As was usual for Thembu royalty, he attended a Wesleyan School and College. The bright, young Nelson Mandela completed his Junior Certificate in only 2 years instead of 3 before moving onto College in Fort Beaufort. In college, he took an interest in running and boxing.

At the University

While attending Fort Hare University pursuing Bachelor of Arts degree, Nelson Mandela met two men—Oliver Tambo and Kaiser 'K.D' Matanzima—who were to become his close friends for life.

Mandela, however, did not complete his degree. A year after attending college, he became involved with the Student Representative Council and their boycott against university policies. This is the first recorded representation of Mandela's political activism. He was told to leave the college.

Not long after this, Mandela refused an arranged marriage proposal and 'ran away' to Johannesburg. He started working as a guard at a mine but was dismissed when it was found that he was a royal runaway. He then completed his degree through correspondence while working as a clerk. He then moved on to study law at the University of Witwatersrand. While studying there Mandela met three influential people—Harry Schwarz, Joe Slovo, Ruth First—who also became anti-apartheid activists. While still studying law, he again entered politics in earnest and entered the African National

Apartheid *a policy where the blacks were rigidly separated and discriminated from the whites*

Boycott *a group of people joining and refusing to buy or sell something*

Congress in 1943. Once again, he left the university without completing his graduation.

Mandela during his college days

Young Mandela, born amid royalty, understood the meaning of equality. So, he started using his knowledge, and beliefs to fight for equality and justice for not only South Africans but for people everywhere.

Early Political Life

Mandela was influenced by the ideals of Mahatma Gandhi. In 1947, Mandela was elected as the secretary to the youth leadership of ANC. The ANCYL aimed to attain full citizenship and direct parliamentary representation of all South Africans. The policy making process paid special attention to the redistribution of the land, trade union rights, education and culture. Mandela, who was a co–author of the policy document, aspired to achieve free and compulsory education for all children, as well as mass education for adults. The ANC launched its Campaign for the Defiance of Unjust Laws in 1952, and Mandela travelled to propagate the campaign. Though he had always avoided violence, he was charged and brought to trial for his role in the campaign.

He was given a suspended prison sentence. He was prohibited from attending gatherings and was confined to Johannesburg for six months. In 1952, Mandela and his followers prepared a plan that would enable the leaders of the movement to maintain dynamic contact among themselves without recourse to public meetings. The plan was called M-Plan, named after Mandela.

Defiance *it is an open refusal to obey someone or something*

Anti-apartheid Movement

Mandela began his political career in 1950. It would take another 44 years till he will become the president of South Africa. All these years, he worked hard to eradicate apartheid and racism in South Africa. In 1952, Mandela was elected as the deputy president of the African National Congress (ANC). It was then that he decided to bureaucratically eradicate apartheid and started the anti-apartheid movement.

The anti-apartheid movement was the first successful transnational social movement in the world. The movement started when a massive turnout by rural Afrikaners gave Rev. Daniel Malan's Nationalist Party a majority of five seats in the whites-only Parliament of South Africa on May 26, 1948. The Nationalists won on a racist platform. They won on the white fears of the 'black threat' and promised to establish strict 'apartheid' policies to counter this fear. What is unique about this movement is the amount of international support it got from governments, organizations and individuals from around the world!

Racism *a doctrine that promotes the idea that one race is superior as compared to other races*

There were two main aspects of the anti-apartheid movement: the internal campaign to destabilize the racist apartheid regime in South Africa, and the external campaign for political, economic, and cultural sanctions. At the heart of the movement was the struggle of black Africans to end white supremacy in South Africa. This struggle became a catalyst for actions at the international level and as well as the crucial link that gave coherence to the movement as a whole. The internal struggle within South Africa was the movement's core and it acted as catalyst for regional and international support movements.

Protestors protesting during the apartheid period

Sanction an official order passed against a country which limits its trade. It is done to make a country agree to do something

The movement first tried nonviolent direct-action tactics under the leadership of the African National Congress (ANC), the South African Communist Party (SACP), the Indian National Congress (INC) and the Pan Africanist Congress (PAC). On May 1, 1950, this coalition organized a national strike to oppose the Suppression of Communism Act. Thousands of workers across South Africa boycotted their jobs. The government sent troops to suppress the strike and 18 workers died in the events that followed. However, the undeterred coalition called for another strike on June 26. Once again, workers joined the strike in large numbers.

These strikes were followed by mass civil-disobedience campaigns of 1952-1953 known collectively as the 'Campaign of Defiance of Unjust Laws.' Between June and December 1952, thousands of activists were arrested for defying petty apartheid laws, such as 'whites only' drinking fountains, train compartments, and waiting rooms. ANC's Nelson Mandela made hundreds of speeches across the country urging black people to defy apartheid laws. In response, the government shot at the demonstrators, and arrested them.

Arrest

South Africa's most wanted man, Mandela, was arrested when he was returning from a six-month clandestine trip through Africa and to London where he garnered support for the ANC's armed wing, 'Umkhonto we Sizwe.' At the end of his trip, Mandela was returning to Johannesburg on Sunday, August 5, 1962, with fellow activist Cecil Williams when the police stopped them and Mandela was arrested. He was charged with leaving the country without a passport and inciting workers to strike. He went on trial in Pretoria on October 15, 1962. On November 7, 1962, he was sentenced to five years of imprisonment.

No sooner had Mandela gone into imprisonment that the police raided Liliesleaf Farm in Rivonia where the members of ANC met. The top members of the ANC were arrested along with many documents related to their plans and actions. They all stood trial for sabotage in what became known as the 'Rivonia Trial'. Documents related to Mandela's plans were also found and he too was once again brought to court on charges of sabotage. On June 11, 1964 Mandela, Walter

Clandestine *something done in secrecy or kept a secret, sometimes to deceive*
Sabotage *a deliberate damage done to machines, transport and other equipment so that the enemy is unable to use them*

Sisulu, Ahmed Kathrada, Raymond Mhlaba, Denis Goldberg, Govan Mbeki, Andrew Mlangeni and Elias Motsoaledi were convicted. The next day they were all sentenced to life imprisonment and were sent to Robben Island. All of them, however, were released in the course of few years except Mandela. He became free from Victor Verster Prison in 1990 after 27 years, 6 months and 5 days.

The Rivonia Trial and Lilliesleaf Farm

After the ANC was banned, its leaders decided to form an underground wing of the ANC called Umkhonto we Sizwe or the MK (meaning spear of the Nation). The MK was formed to 'be at the front line of the people's defence...' and to fight against the government's policies related to racial oppression.'

Between December 1961 and July 1963, MK units undertook just over 200 operations, which were mainly intended to damage public facilities.

The old Lilliesleaf farmhouse on an isolated location was a perfect hideout for the banned members of the ANC. Here, they could discuss and

Banned the act of stopping someone or something from doing something legally

develop their next move and strategies. Acting on the information provided by Gerard Ludi, an agent for the government, the police raided Lilliesleaf Farm on July 11, 1963. When the police burst in, they found virtually the entire leadership of the MK.

Along with the banned members, the police found hundreds of incriminating documents. After the raid more arrests followed. At the time of their arrest, MK's commanders had met to discuss Operation Mayibuye, a proposal prepared by Joe Slovo and Mbeki for a guerrilla insurgency.

The scheme envisaged an initial stage of dispersed rural operations that would be supported by externally derived supplies. The scheme's prospects would depend on the collaboration of foreign governments capable of transporting guerrillas into South Africa by air and by sea.

At the time of the Rivonia raid both Slovo and Mbeki believed that they had already convinced their colleagues to go ahead with the scheme. Slovo had left South Africa two months before, travelling to the ANC's exile headquarters to brief Oliver

Incriminating to make it look like as if someone has done something wrong

Tambo about the plan. Tambo was enthusiastic about the project, according to Slovo. However, during the trial Mandela along with other MK leaders maintained that Operation Mayibuye was just a proposal and an impractical one at that.

Mandela arrested

When the Rivonia raid occurred Mandela was already in prison sentenced for five years. During the Lilliesleaf raid the police had discovered documentation implicating Mandela in MK's activities, including notes he had made from his readings about guerrilla warfare and a diary he had kept during his African trip. In October 1963, ten accused, including Nelson Mandela, Walter Sisulu and Govan Mbeki, appeared in what subsequently came to be known as the Rivonia Trial.

The Rivonia Trial

Before the trial, for nearly ninety days, the arrested men were interrogated and detained in solitary confinement. The trial started in October 1963 in Pretoria before Justice Quartus de Wet. Ten defendants were brought to trial and charged on four counts. The alleged offenses were: (1) recruiting persons for training in the preparation and use of explosives and in guerrilla warfare for the purpose of violent revolution and committing acts of sabotage, (2) conspiring to commit the aforementioned acts and to aid foreign military units when they invaded the Republic, (3) acting in these ways to further the objects of communism, and (4) soliciting and receiving money for these purposes from sympathizers in Algeria, Ethiopia, Liberia, Nigeria, Tunisia, and elsewhere.

At the trial, Nelson Mandela chose to make a statement from the dock rather than from the witness stand. He was questioned about his entries in his dairy, where he had indicated that the ANC's plans for guerrilla warfare were already quite advanced by early 1962.

In the opening passages of his defence, Mandela admitted that he had helped to form MK and he had helped to plan its sabotage campaign. 'Civil war', though, remained an optional 'last resort', one that had yet to be decided upon. The ANC had formed an alliance with the multiracial Communist Party, though the two organizations did not share 'a complete community of interests'.

Mandela said that MK was an African movement, fighting for dignity, for decent livelihoods, and for equal rights. He ended his statement with an exposition of his personal standpoint:

'Africans want to be paid a living wage. Africans want to perform work which they are capable of ... Africans want to be allowed to live where they obtain work, and not be endorsed out of an area because they were not born there. Africans want

to be allowed to own land in places where they work ... Africans want to be part of the general population and not confined to living in their own ghettoes...

Above all, we want equal political rights ... I know it sounds revolutionary to the whites in this country, because the majority of voters will be African. But this fear cannot be allowed to stand in the way of the only solution which will guarantee racial harmony and freedom for all...

During my lifetime I have dedicated myself to the struggle of the African people. I have fought against white domination, and I have fought against black domination. I have cherished the ideal of a democratic and free society in which all persons live together in harmony and with equal opportunities. It is an ideal which I hope to live for and to achieve. But if needs be it is an ideal for which I am prepared to die'.

This eloquent testimonial was reproduced in every newspaper worldwide. The speech continues to be the most definitive expression of liberal African nationalism, cementing Mandela's iconic status in South Africa and - importantly for the ANC - internationally.

Mandela in prison

June 12, 1964 - The Trial Ends

However, the court sentenced eight of the convicted to life imprisonment. Mandela, Sisulu, Mbeki, Motsoaledi, Mlangeni, and Goldberg were found guilty on all four counts. They were sent to Robben Island.

The Impact of the Trial

By imprisoning leaders of MK and the ANC, the government had successfully broken the strength of the ANC inside South Africa. However, at the same time the verdict of the trial faced international criticism of apartheid. The United Nations condemned the trial and began taking steps to introduce sanctions on South Africa. Over the next few years there were a few acts of sabotage while the ANC worked on how to infiltrate South Africa now that the top leaders were in prison. It seemed that for the time being the government had been able to crush the resistance.

Though Mandela and the top leaders of the ANC were in prison their struggle to fight against apartheid continued. While in prison Mandela studied from the University of London by correspondence and completed his degree in law. While Mandela was still in prison, several attempts were made to assassinate him but all of them failed. In 1982, Mandela was moved to Pollsmoor Prison. It was done so to reduce his influence on the young black activists. During this time he was allowed increasing contact with his wife, Winnie Mandela,

Assassinate to suddenly kill a politically important person

and their two daughters.

President P.W. Botha, in 1985, offered Mandela his freedom on the condition that he unconditionally rejects violence as a political weapon. His ministers had told him that Mandela would never seek his freedom by asking his organization to give up the armed struggle. As expected, Mandela refused the offer. His daughter Zindzi read his statement where he said, "What freedom am I being offered while the organisation of the people remains banned? Only free men can negotiate. A prisoner cannot enter into contracts."

Over the next four years, for the first time, discussions took place to bring an end to this struggle of the black people. In 1988, Mandela was shifted to Victor Verster Prison. Several restrictions on him were also lifted. Meanwhile during this time international pressure had been mounting on the South African government to release Nelson Mandela. Also discussions to end apartheid continued in earnest while he was in Victor Verster Prison.

Nelson Mandela released

Release

In 1989, Botha was replaced by F. W. De Klerk as president of South Africa. Soon, he announced Mandela's release in February 1990. Meanwhile negotiations continued. Government representatives preferred to negotiate with Mandela alone. Mandela outlined the negotiated issues as 'the armed struggle, the ANC's alliance with the Communist Party, the goal of majority rule, and the idea of racial reconciliation.' The government representatives still feared that the ANC might attempt 'blanket nationalization of

Reconciliation to put an end to a disagreement and start again at a relationship
Negotiation discussion among persons or groups trying to agree on something

the South African economy' as stated in the ANC's Freedom Charter. But the international pressure was mounting.

At last, the ANC, PAC, and SACP were legalized on February 2, 1990, and Nelson Mandela was released from Victor Vester Prison on February 11, 1990. The event was broadcasted live all across the globe. After his release, Mandela addressed the nation where he stated that he would continue to work towards attaining peace and reconciliation with the white community.

Negotiations to End Apartheid in South Africa

The apartheid system in South Africa was ended through a series of negotiations between 1990 and 1993 and through unilateral steps by the de Klerk government. These negotiations took place between the governing National Party, the African National Congress of which Nelson Mandela was president, and a wide variety of other political organisations. The negotiations resulted in South Africa's first multi-racial election, which was won by the African National Congress.

Mandela's leadership through the negotiations, as well as his relationship with President F.W. de Klerk, was recognised and they were jointly awarded the Nobel Peace Prize in 1993.

Presidency of South Africa

Four years of tireless activism finally brought apartheid to an end. For the first time, multi-racial presidential elections were held in South Africa in 1994. Nelson Mandela, president of the African National Congress and recipient of the 1993 Nobel Prize for Peace, won the election. He became South Africa's first black, freely elected president. Throughout his term, Mandela worked to bring the white and black communities together and made efforts for national and international reconciliation.

Marriage and Family

From the time Mandela began his fight against apartheid and for equality, it was apparent that his wife needed to be strong. Mandela has had three wives in his life, marrying the last on his 80th birthday.

Nelson Mandela has fathered 6 children. He fathered four children from his first marriage to Evelyn Mase and 2 children from his second wife Winnie Madikizela.

Mandela with his family

Both of Mandela's daughters from his first marriage were named Makazawie. The eldest died at nine months and the next Makazawie was named in her honour. Madiba Thembikile (Thembi) was killed in a car crash when he was 25 (1969). Nelson Mandela was in prison at the time and was not permitted to attend his son's funeral. Makgatho died of

AIDS in 2005. Nelson Mandela has been active in expressing his views on HIV/ AIDS and the 46664 AIDS campaign is named after his prison number.

Nelson and Evelyn were married for 13 years, splitting up in 1957. She died in 2004. In 1958 Nelson married Winnie Madikizela. While much of their marriage was spent apart as Nelson was in prison, Winnie Mandela became a strong political figure herself. Mandela and Winnie have 2 girls Zenani (Zeni) and Zindziswa (Zindzi).

Due to both political and personal strain, Nelson and Winnie divorced in 1994. In 1998, on his 80th birthday Nelson married his third wife, Graca Machel, widow of the former Mozambican president. Nelson Mandela currently lives in Qunu. While he does have several houses around the world, Nelson Mandela's place is in his birth region of Transkei.

Retirement

Nelson Mandela took retirement from politics on August 19, 1999. Since then he had dedicated himself to The Nelson Mandela Foundation which continues to capture his vision, work and ideals. The Foundation embodies the spirit of reconciliation and social justice and celebrates the life of Nelson Mandela.

In November 2006, the Foundation's Board of Trustees approved a new vision for the Foundation with aims to consolidate and spread Mr Mandela's legacy.

The Nelson Mandela Foundation also convenes dialogue around critical social issues, while continuing to provide support to its founder.

After his retirement as President in 1999, Mandela went on to become an advocate for a variety of social, and human rights organisations. He used his status to raise awareness against important issues.

Health

As his health declined, Mandela chose to retire from public life in 2004. He restricted his public appearances but he was too large a figure to simply disappear. His name has been used to promote charitable ventures close to his heart such as the Nelson Mandela Invitational charity golf tournament, raising millions of rand for children's charities since its establishment in 2000.

AIDS Engagement

The fight against AIDS was one of Mandela's primary concerns and he used his status to raise awareness about the issue on the global stage. He backed the 46664 campaign which was named after his prison number. He appealed to people to talk about AIDS with an open mind. His son Makgatho Mandela had died of Aids in 2005 and Mandela used the occasion to tell people that talking about the condition is the only way to break away from the stigma.

The Elders

In 2007 he brought together elder statesmen, peace activists and human rights advocates including Kofi Annan, Jimmy Carter, Ela Bhatt, Gro Harlem Brundtland and Li Zhaoxing under a non-governmental organisation dubbed 'The Elders'. The aim of the organisation was to combine the elders' collective wisdom and to use it to solve some of the world's problems.

The Elders

In November 2009, Mandela's contributions to the world were rewarded with a unique gesture by the United Nations General Assembly. It was announced that July 18, his birthday, would be from now known as Mandela Day. The recipient of hundreds of awards and honorary recognitions, including the Nobel Peace Prize, Mandela continues to influence various world activities.

Awards and Honours

Nelson Mandela has received more than a thousand awards over the past four decades for his struggle for democracy, equality and learning. He won international respect for bridging the black and white races. Leading a life that symbolizes the triumph of the human spirit over man's inhumanity to man, Nelson Mandela accepted the Nobel Peace Prize in 1993 along with F. W. De Klerk on behalf of South Africans who had suffered so much so that there could be peace in the world. His life and works continue to inspire people around the world.

WINSTON CHURCHILL

Winston Churchill was an exceptional orator, an artist and Nobel Prize winner for literature. Yet, he is mostly known as a British statesman who led United Kingdom through World War II. He twice served as the prime minister of the United Kingdom.

The Child

Winston Churchill was born into the privileged world of British aristocracy on November 30, 1874 in his grandfather's house Blenheim Palace in Marlborough. His father, Lord Randolph Churchill, was a member of the British parliament while his mother, Jennie Jerome, was the daughter of an American business tycoon, Leonard Jerome.

Winston's childhood was not a particularly happy one. Like many Victorian parents, Lord and Lady Randolph Churchill were distant. The family Nanny, Mrs Elizabeth Everest, became a surrogate mother to Winston and his younger brother, John S Churchill, who was born six years after Winston. Winston was close to his nanny and stayed in touch with her until her death in 1895. He was initially educated in a boarding school. In 1887, he was accepted in the prestigious Harrow School where besides the subjects, he learnt military tactics. After passing from Harrow, he was accepted in the Royal Military College, Sandhurst in 1893.

The Soldier

After passing out of Sandhurst in December 1894, Churchill was commissioned as a cavalry officer. While returning home after seven months of training, Churchill travelled to Cuba to have a firsthand had experience of battle as the Spanish troops put down a rebellion. He not only enjoyed the experience but decided to be a war correspondent for *The Daily Graphic*.

In 1897, Churchill went on to see more action on the North West Frontier of India. Once again, he did not fight but became a war correspondent, this time for the *Daily Telegraph*. He rode his grey pony along the skirmish lines in full view of the enemy. "Foolish perhaps," he told his mother, "but I play for high stakes and given an audience there is no act too daring and too noble." Churchill wrote about his experiences in his first book *The Story of the Malakand Field Force* (1898). He soon became an accomplished war reporter, getting paid large sums for stories he sent to the press. This was the beginning of a long writing career.

Portrait of Winston Churchill

In 1899, Churchill had his first brush with his long political career. He was invited to be a Conservative Party Candidate in Oldham constituency. Though Churchill lost the seat but his vigorous campaigning impressed everyone.

So in 1899, he once again went as a war correspondent for the *Morning Post* to South Africa. Never been able to resist a fight, he took part in the defence of an armoured train which had been ambushed by the Boers. He was captured and treated as a prisoner of war. However, Churchill managed to escape with a few weeks and returned to Durban. Churchill was hailed as a hero for his exceptional escape. He also wrote and had his experiences published as a book **London to Ladysmith via Pretoria** (1990).

He obtained a military commission from the Commander-in-Chief but continued to act as a war correspondent, enjoying many further adventures. It was also during his many adventures that he decided to make policies and not just follow them. So, he returned to England and ran for the seat of Member of Parliament in 1900. He was 25 years old at that time.

The Politician

Running for the seat of MP was just the beginning of Churchill's long political career. He was first

Ambush is to remain hidden and then suddenly attack someone

elected to parliament in 1900 shortly before the death of Queen Victoria. He took his seat in the House of Commons as the Conservative Member for Oldham in February 1901 and made his first speech merely four days later. He quickly became known for his energy and being outspoken. But after only four years as a Conservative, he realized that he did not share the views of the conservatives and joined the Liberals. This move to join the liberal party happened in 1904.

Churchill rose swiftly within the Liberal ranks. In 1905, the liberal party won the national elections. Then, Churchill was made Under-Secretary of State at the Colonial Office. His dedication and hard work earned him respect and reputation and in 1908, he earned the seat of a cabinet minister-President of the Board of Trade. He was promoted to the position of Home Secretary in 1910. Then in 1911, he was First Lord of the Admiralty. Holding this position meant that he controlled the British navy.

Now that he was in a position of power, he started raising his suspicions regarding the increasing military strength of Germany. He spent the next three years working tirelessly to strengthen the British navy. However, his political career wasn't all smooth sailing. He was often criticized for his blunders and some thought that his genius lacked judgment.

Though, when World War I broke out he was greatly praised for strengthening the British forces. The chief setback of his career occurred in 1915 when, as First Lord of the Admiralty, he sent a naval force to the Dardanelles during World War I in an attempt to knock Turkey out of the war and to outflank Germany on a continental scale. The campaign which was supposed to be a joint naval and cavalry attack went badly as was least expected. This expedition set out at the command of Churchill turned out be a disaster and greatly harmed the reputation of Winston Churchill. As everyone, statesmen and civilians turned against Churchill, he was swiftly moved out of government.

Churchill was greatly saddened by the turn of events. Though he remained a member of parliament but there was never enough for him to do and he was a very active man. It was during this time that Winston Churchill learnt to paint and devoted himself to learning it. He remained out of politics for nearly 2 years. However, Churchill could not be kept out of power for long. In 1917, he was once again invited back to active politics and appointed as Minister of Munitions. Then in 1918, he was given the position of the Secretary of State for War and Air. From this position, he could ask all the British soldiers to come home.

The next decade brought with it many ups and down for Churchill. In the beginning of the decade, Churchill lost his MP seat. Then, between 1922 and 1924 Churchill felt himself leaning towards the Conservative Party. So, he left the Liberals and joined the Conservative Party. In 1924, he again won an MP seat, this time as a conservative. To his great surprise, Churchill was appointed Chancellor of the Exchequer by Stanley Baldwin, an office in which he served from 1924 to 1929. Apart from his busy political career, Churchill continued to write. It was during this time that he wrote his six-volume work on World War I, **The World Crisis** (1911 - 1918).

Then after the general elections in 1919, the Labour Party went out of power. During the next ten years, Churchill became more and more isolated in politics and he found the experience of perpetual opposition deeply frustrating. Though he held his MP seat but he did not held onto a position of power. But he did not slow down. He continued to write and paint. He also gave speeches where he warned about Germany's growing power and the drawbacks of Chamberlain's appeasement policy.

But due to the blunders he made during the decade, no one paid heed to his warnings. After the Munich crisis, however, Churchill's prophecies were seen to be coming true and when war broke out on September 3, 1939 Prime Minister Neville Chamberlain appointed him First Lord of the Admiralty. So, nearly twenty-five years after he had left the post in great disappointment, the Navy sent out a signal to the Fleet: "Winston is back".

The War Leader

For the first nine months of the conflict, Churchill proved that he was, as Admiral Fisher had once said, "a war man". Chamberlain was not a man

Appeasement to maintain peace and calm by giving someone what they want

adept in military tactics and soon took a step back. Consequently the failures of the Norwegian Campaign were blamed on the Prime Minister rather than the belligerent First Lord. So, when Chamberlain resigned after criticisms in the House of Commons, Churchill became leader of a coalition government. So, as Germany attacked France on May 10, 1945, Chamberlain resigned as prime minister. The same day King George VI asked Churchill to become the Prime Minister of Britain. It was the finest hour for both Winston and Britain.

Inspecting the destruction of a cathedral during the World War

When the German armies conquered France and Britain awaited the onslaught, Churchill embodied his country's will to resist. He gave a number of speeches to boost the morale of the people and inspire them to keep fighting an unrelenting army. When asked exactly what Churchill did to win the war, Clement Attlee, the Labour leader who served in the coalition government, replied: "Talk about it." Churchill talked incessantly, in private as well as in public.

Churchill devoted much of his energy in trying to persuade American President Roosevelt to support him in the war. He wrote the President a number of letters and soon they developed a strong relation. And he managed to get American help in the Atlantic, where until 1943 Britain's lifeline to the New World was always under severe threat from German U-Boats.

It was also during this time, that Churchill as he sought help from the United States, also had to seek the Soviet Union as his ally. Though Churchill hated the communists, he without any hesitations sent aid to the soviet soldiers and defended Stalin in public. "If Hitler invaded Hell," he once remarked,

"I would at least make a favourable reference to the Devil in the House of Commons."

In December 1941, six months after Hitler had invaded Russia, Japan attacked Pearl Harbor. The war in Europe and Asia had now become global. But with the might of America on the Allied side there could be no doubt about the outcome of the war. Churchill was jubilant, remarking when he heard the news of Pearl Harbor: "So we have won after all!"

Stalin, Roosevelt and Churchill

However, America's entry into the war also caused Churchill problems; as he said, the only thing worse than fighting a war with allies is fighting a war without them.

It soon became apparent that Churchill was the littlest of the "Big Three". At the Teheran Conference in November, 1943, he said, the "poor little English donkey was squeezed between the great Russian bear and the mighty American buffalo, yet only he knew the way home."

In June 1944, the Allies forces invaded Normandy and the Americans were clearly in command. General Eisenhower pushed across Northern Europe on a broad front. Germany was crushed between this advance and the Russian steamroller. On May 8, 1945 Britain accepted Germany's surrender and celebrated Victory. Churchill told a huge crowd in Whitehall: "This is your victory." The people shouted: "No, it is yours", and Churchill conducted them in the singing of Land of Hope and Glory. That evening he broadcast to the nation urging the defeat of Japan and paying fulsome homage to the Crown.

Churchill won accolades from everywhere even from his critics. But the tables soon turned against him. Meanwhile, though victory was widely celebrated throughout Britain, the war in the Far East went on for three more months before it ended. The atomic bombing of Hiroshima and Nagasaki finally brought the global conflict to a conclusion. It was at this moment that at the time of his greatest triumph, he tasted bitter defeat.

The Elder Statesman

Soon, it was time for elections in Britain. Churchill expected to win the election of 1945. Everything from opinion polls, cartoons in newspapers and the adulations he received all pointed towards his victory during the elections. However, Churchill himself ruined his victory celebrations. From the beginning, he accused the Labour Party of putting the party before country and he later said that Socialists could not rule without a political police, a Gestapo. Churchill was hopeful for his victory but things turned out differently. When the outcome of the elections came out, Churchill was shocked by the scale of his defeat in the election. For a time he lapsed into depression, while sympathetic letters from friends did little to dispel it.

Soon, however, Churchill re-entered politics, taking an active part in political life from the opposition benches and once again gave many speeches after the victory over Japan. In defeat Churchill had always been defiant, but in victory he favoured magnanimity. Within a couple of years he was calling for a partnership between a "spiritually great France and a spiritually great Germany" as the basis for the re-creation of "the European family". When the memories were still fresh in the world's eye, Churchill announced the beginning of the Cold War. At Fulton, Missouri, in 1946, he pointed to the new threat posed by the Soviet Union and declared that an iron curtain had descended across Europe. Only by keeping the alliance between the English-speaking peoples strong, he maintained, could the Communist tyranny be resisted.

After losing another election in 1950, Churchill gained victory at the polls, the next year. Publicly Churchill called for "several years of quiet steady administration". This is something that he managed to achieve. But he failed to arrange a summit with

Cold War a highly unfriendly relation between two countries without actually fighting each other

the Russians. Later, he suffered a serious stroke and the news of it was kept away from the public and the congress. Under these conditions, Churchill resigned from his premiership in April 1955.

"I am ready to meet my Maker," Churchill had said on his seventy-fifth birthday; "whether my Maker is prepared for the great ordeal of meeting me is another matter". Churchill remained a member of parliament, though an inactive one. It was in 1963 that he announced his retirement from politics. His retirement had a great effect during the general election the following year.

Churchill spent the time of his retirement in Chartwell as well as at his home in Hyde Park Gate in London. On January 15, 1965, Churchill suffered a serious stroke. He died at his London home on January 24, 1965, nine days later. He received the greatest state funeral given to a commoner. He was buried in Bladon churchyard beside his parents and within sight of his birthplace, Blenheim Palace.

The Family Man

In the autumn of 1908, Churchill, then a rising Liberal politician, married Clementine Hozier,

Churchill's State funeral

granddaughter of the 10th Earl of Airlie. Their marriage was a long and happy one, though there were often quarrels. Clementine was high principled and highly strung; Winston was stubborn and ambitious. His work invariably came first but he was greatly devoted to his children.

Winston and Clementine's first child, Diana, was born in 1909. Diana was a naughty little girl and even when she had grown into an adult she caused great trouble for her parents. In 1932, she married John Bailey. Their marriage, however remained unsuccessful and they divorced in 1935. She later remarried and had three children through that marriage. But that marriage too failed. In the end, Diana committed suicide in 1963 after several nervous breakdowns.

The Churchills' second child and only son, Randolph, was born in 1911. He was exceptionally handsome and rumbustious. During the 1930s Randolph stood for parliament several times but he failed to get in. He, however, did serve as Conservative Member of Parliament for Preston between 1940 and 1945. He later became a successful journalist and began writing the official biography of Winston Churchill, his father during the 1960s. Randolph was married twice, first in 1939 to Pamela Digby by whom he had a son, Winston, and secondly in 1948 to June Osborne by whom he had a daughter, Arabella. Neither marriage succeeded.

The life of Sarah, the Churchills' third child, born in 1914, was no happier than that of her elder siblings. He took up dramatics as her career which flourished for a time. Sarah's charm and vitality were also apparent in her private life, but her first two marriages proved unsuccessful and she was widowed soon after her third. Her first husband was a music hall artist Vic Oliver whom she married against her parents' wishes. Her second was Anthony Beauchamp but this marriage did not last.

In 1918, Clementine Churchill gave birth to a third girl, Marigold. In 1921, Marigold contracted septicaemia while on a seaside holiday with the governess. When she died Winston was grief-stricken. The following September, the Churchills' fifth and last child, Mary, was born. Unlike her older siblings, Mary was a pillar of support for her parents, especially her mother. In 1947, she married Christopher Soames; who was then

Assistant Military Attaché in Paris and later had a successful parliamentary and diplomatic career. They had a long, happy marriage.

The Private Man

Churchill's enormous reserves of energy and his legendary ability to exist on very little sleep gave him time to pursue a wide variety of interests outside politics.

Churchill loved gambling and he even lost quiet an amount giving a setback to the finances of his family. Besides gambling, Churchill continued to write throughout his life. Apart from his major works, which concerned the great wars and one on his ancestor, Churchill wrote several articles for newspapers and magazines and even wrote his speeches. His last big book was the **History of the English-Speaking Peoples**, which he had begun in 1938. It was published in the 1950s. For his contribution to literature through his works, Churchill received in 1953 the Nobel Prize for Literature.

Decades ago, Churchill had taken up painting as an antidote to the anguish he felt over the Dardanelles disaster. Painting proved to be a source of solace and he was rarely seen during that time without his brush and canvas.

In the summer of 1922, while on the lookout for a suitable country house, Churchill caught sight of a property near Westerham in Kent. He liked the property so much that he instantly decided to buy it. Despite Clementine's initial lack of enthusiasm for the dilapidated and neglected house, Chartwell became a much loved house by the Churchill's.

Churchill was born into the world of hunting, shooting and fishing and throughout his life they were to prove spasmodic distractions. But it was hunting and polo, first learned as a young cavalry officer in India, that he enjoyed most of all.

Among Winston's closest friends were Professor Lindemann and the "the three B's", Birkenhead, Beaverbook, Bracken. The Churchills' entertained widely Charlie Chaplin, Albert Einstein and Lawrence of Arabia who were among their guests. Churchill is widely regarded as one of the most influential Britons in the world. He was also the honorary citizen of the United States, an honour given to him by F.D. Roosevelt in 1963.

Antidote it is a remedy that controls the effects of a poison or a disease

MARTIN LUTHER KING JR.

Martin Luther King, Jr. dedicated his life to the African American Civil Right Movement and used nonviolent means to pursue them. An international icon, a clergyman, an activist, any reference to American liberalism is incomplete without mentioning him.

His first encounter with racism came when he was six years old. That encounter willed him to change the American society making it a better and fairer place to live in.

Early Childhood, Education and Family

Martin Luther King, Jr. was born on January 15, 1929, in his maternal grandparents' large Victorian house on Auburn Avenue in Atlanta, Georgia. His father, Reverend Martin Luther King Sr. was the pastor of Ebenezer Baptist Church in Atlanta. He was originally named Michael but later his name was changed to Martin. He had two siblings, an elder sister Willie Christine and a younger brother Alfred Daniel Williams.

Being a minister's son, and growing up in a loving environment, young Martin was far away from the economic troubles the black community was facing during the years of the Great Depression. The family was financially secure and they owned their own house.

Their house and everyone in it was centered around his father and the church. At age four, Martin frequently sang gospel songs accompanied by his mother on the piano. He was exceptionally good at it. He thus became so popular that he was occasionally booked to sing for revival meetings

Gospel four books in The Bible about the life and teaching of Jesus Christ

and conventions. As he grew up, he had better education than his counterparts of the same race.

His first brush with racism came when he was six. Among his playmates were two white boys, sons of the neighbourhood grocer. At the time of schooling, the two boys joined the whites' school and gradually they were discouraged to play with each other. One day, when Martin went to play with the boys, he was curtly told by their mother, "We are white and you are coloured, and you can't play together anymore." Shocked and with tears in his eyes, Martin went to his mother. She consoled Martin and told him about the treatment of his race throughout the decades.

Martin grew up in a politically influential family as both his father and grandfather served as ministers. He learnt his first lessons from his mother who was a school teacher. As he grew up, he was seen as a mixture of his father's volatile, quick temper and his mother's composure.

Martin Luther attended Booker T. Washington High School in Atlanta. Though he was an average student, he managed to skip ninth and twelfth grade. He entered Morehouse College at 15 and earned Bachelor's of Arts degree, in Sociology from the college. He then graduated with Bachelor of Divinity degree, from Crozer Theological Seminary in Chester, Pennsylvania. He then pursued doctoral studies in systematic theology and earned PhD degree from Boston University.

King was supremely intelligent and had great intellectual potential. At on point, he thought about teaching theology at a university or seminary.

However, it was at Morehouse, an all black campus, where he got to speak about and listen to race related questions openly. The students criticized the system and talked about their future course of action. Some of these wanted to join societies that held radical views but Martin thought unlike them. He, instead, took the membership of the Intercollegiate Council which had student representatives from both white and black groups.

Later, while he had a summer job as a stockroom helper at the Southern Spring Bed Mattress Company, he had another encounter with the whites. Working together, he realized that they

Theology it is the field of study where one learns about religion and beliefs

shared the same feelings and concerns except for their wages. Money he understood was not just the root cause of evil but of racism in particular.

King with wife Coretta and their children

Though King was born in the late twenties, at the time of the Great Depression, but in his writing he chiefly focuses on his experiences of his family life and his relationship with the church. King writes fondly and nostalgically about his family and "that intimate relationship that existed between us in childhood" which included his siblings and maternal grandmother who lived with his family. He recalls listening to her stories as part of the 'congenial home situation'.

He recalls that he was introduced to his future wife; Coretta, by a friend in Boston over the phone. Coretta's life changed when she decided to marry Martin. She first met him when she was studying music at Boston University and had started her career as a concert singer. She had not thought that she would a preacher's wife. She recalls, "Martin was an unusual person...He was so alive and so much fun to be with. He had the strength that he imparted to me and others that he met."

Martin and Coretta were married on June 18, 1953 on the lawn of her parent's home in Marion, Alabama. The ceremony was performed by

Nostalgic a feeling of sadness and happiness when one thinks of happier times

Martin's father. Together, Martin and Coretta had four children.

In 1954, at 25 years of age, Martin became the pastor of Dexter Avenue Baptist Church in Montgomery, Alabama.

Influences of Thurman, Gandhi and Rustin

Martin Luther King, Jr. as he grew up saw the racial discrimination around him. He was determined to remove it. He remembered that his mother had once told him, "You must never feel that you are less than anybody else. You must always feel that you are somebody."

While he was studying, Martin was influenced by his father's classmate at Morehouse College and civil rights leader, theologian and educator Howard Thurman. Thurman, an author, theologian, educator and civil rights leader had grown up in the segregated south. The first black dean at a white university and cofounder of the first interracial church in the US, Thurman was a spiritual advisor to Martin. He constantly reminded people of the social responsibility that emerged from religious faith.

Segregate *to separate and treat someone or a group differently from others*
Civil Rights *include the right to vote, equal treatment in spite of someone's sex, race or religion*

King was also influenced by Henry David Thoreau and his theories on how to use non-violent resistance to achieve social change. Thoreau was an American author, poet, abolitionist and a philosopher. His philosophy of civil disobedience had influenced various figures including Leo Tolstoy, Mahatma Gandhi and King Jr.

It was later that Gandhi's ideology influenced Martin. He was particularly struck by Gandhi's words, "Through our pain we will make them see their injustice". Gandhi was no academic but a man of action but he avoided using violent means to achieve his ends. The means were as important as the ends. The way a conflict is conducted defines the fate of the judgment to a great extent.

Inspired by Gandhi's success with non-violent activism, King visited India in 1959. The visit proved insightful as it helped Martin in committing himself to America's struggle for civil rights through non-violent means. He studied Gandhi's teachings and realized that power and social change can be an outcome of love and truth. Gandhi's search for truth convinced him that truth can be attained through tolerance and concern for others. Courage was required to practice non violence and it appeared to be the surest path to help people realize their freedom.

The Montgomery County Bus Strikes

In March 1955, a high school girl named Claudette Colvin was arrested for refusing to give up her seat on a public bus for a white passenger. For the first time, Jim Crow's laws were successfully challenged in the history of Montgomery, Alabama. The laws gave the African Americans separate but equal status which, however, was slightly inferior.

Assertively fighting for her constitutional rights, Claudette recalled years later: "I couldn't get up that day. History kept me stuck to my seat." She was handcuffed and taken to the city hall where she fought her case. The case came in the attention of the boycott leaders. King happened to be a member of the committee from the Birmingham African American community that was investigating the case. Then on December 1, 1955, Rosa Parks was arrested for refusing to give up her seat. Montgomery Bus Boycott followed her arrest, planned and executed by Nixon and King. The boycott lasted for 385 days.

King quickly emerged as the leader who led the boycott movement. The movement became the nation's biggest moral struggle since the Civil War.

In 1958, King said, "I neither started the protest nor suggested it. I simply responded to the call of the people for a spokesman...Montgomery is known as the Cradle of Confederacy. It has been a quiet cradle for a long, long time. But now the cradle is rocking. "

According to the system of segregation, white people who boarded the bus got the front seats. If the bus was full, the blacks were required to vacate the seats for the whites. The Montgomery Bus Boycott was a social and political campaign which opposed the racial segregation on public transport in Alabama. The strike caused a great debt to the transport system. The boycott only ended with the US Supreme Court ruling which said that the segregation on the bases of colour in buses was unconstitutional.

Even before Rosa, E.D. Nixon, president of the local NAACP had been protesting against the segregation. After the arrest of Rosa Parks, Nixon organized a meeting of local ministers at Martin Luther King, Jr.'s church. During this meeting, King was chosen to lead the movement.

On the night of Rosa Parks' arrest, Jo Ann Robinson, head of the Women's Political Council, printed and circulated a flyer throughout Montgomery's black community:

"Another woman has been arrested and thrown in jail because she refused to get up out of her seat on the bus for a white person...This has to be stopped. Negroes have rights too...This woman's case will come up on Monday. We are, therefore, asking every Negro to stay off the buses on Monday in protest of the arrest and trial. Don't ride the buses to work, to town, to school, or anywhere on Monday."

The following morning, a church meeting led by King proposed a citywide boycott of public transit demanding a fixed dividing line for the segregated sections of the buses. This meant that in buses if the white section was full, the blacks won't be asked to give up their seats. They also demanded that black drivers should be employed. The boycott proved extremely effective. Instead of using buses, the commuters started using carpooling. Black taxi drivers started charging the bus fare while some people resorted to cycling, walking, and riding horse-drawn carriages.

The white population reacted by crowding the ranks of the White Citizen's Council. A few incidents of violence including firebombing of King's house and four black Baptist churches were also reported. Later, King was arrested along with others. However, the boycott did more than just fight against racial segregation. The movement led to the beginning of the Civil Rights Movement in the US and brought King under national focus.

King described the movement as "Fifty thousand who took to heart the principle of non-violence, who learned to fight for their rights with the weapon of love, and who, in the process, acquired a new estimate of their own human worth. ... The majority of the people who took part in the year long boycott of the Montgomery's buses were poor and untutored; but they understood the essence of the Montgomery movement. One elderly woman summed it up for the rest. When asked after several weeks of walking whether she was tired, she answered, 'my feet is tired, but my soul is at rest".

The WPC (Women's Political Council) went into action with the arrest of Rosa Parks. Meanwhile, many attempts were made by the racist White Citizens Council to sabotage the boycott including enforcement of a policy of the police arresting any group of black people waiting at pick-up stations along with those volunteering to drive them to their destinations. Telephonic threats were also given to the black citizens.

In the beginning, the black community only wanted the segregation laws to be modified. But when they realized that their demands would not be met they demanded a complete reconstruction of the laws. With time, they demanded that the Jim Crow laws should be removed.

On Feburary 21, 1956, a grand jury of 17 whites and one Black declared the boycott illegal. It then took almost thirteen months of constant struggle which led to the victory that laid the foundation for the Civil Rights Movement.

Southern Christian Leadership Conference

After the boycott movement was successful, Martin Luther became associated with the SCLC (Southern Christian Leadership Conference). It was an organization that fought for civil rights. As a principal organization of the Civil Rights Movement, the SCLC organized and sponsored many protest marches and demonstrations during the late 1950's and 60's. The organization came into being on January 1957 after the success of the Montgomery Bus Boycott. Initially the goal of the organization was to put an end to the racial segregation on the public transport system. However, the goals later changed to end all kinds of segregation. The organization also sought voting rights and other benefits for the African Americans. The organization sought to take the Civil Rights cause out of the courtroom and into the community with the hope that it would be easier to negotiate with the whites.

Battle for Equality

Building on the success of the Montgomery boycott, King organized the Southern Christian Leadership Conference (SCLC). He toured extensively to speak on Civil Rights. In 1960, when he returned from his tour to Atlanta, he supported the civil rights "sit-in" demonstrations. However, the movement failed.

Then in 1963, planning began for a mass protest campaign for Birmingham. King said that Birmingham 'is the most thoroughly segregated big city in the US.' He announced that he would lead the demonstrations in the city. This campaign lasted for a month where the protestors faced many police atrocities. During the campaign more than 3000 protestors including King were arrested and jailed.

President Kennedy then made the congress pass the Civil Rights Act of 1964. The act authorized the federal government to enforce desegregation and outlaw discrimination in publicly owned facilities and employment.

Demonstrations were held by Civil Rights activists in 1965 for a federal voting law to protect the rights of the African Americans. King organized a march from Selma, Alabama to Montgomery. The Voting Rights Act was passed during the same year authorizing federal examiners to register qualified voters and outlaw practices including literacy tests. Later, in 1967, King was seen broadening his horizons to the international arena. He openly opposed the US involvement in the Vietnam War. Then, in 1968, he travelled to Memphis, Tennessee, to support a strike by the city's garbage workers. By then though equality had been maintained but the changes in attitudes towards African Americans were still required.

Letter from Birmingham Jail

In 1963, Martin was arrested and jailed for protesting against the existing segregation laws in Birmingham. In response to these arrests, King drafted a document that became a turning point in the Civil Rights Movement and continues to inspire to fight for racial equality. He then, wrote a letter from Birmingham Jail.

In this document, popularly known as 'Letter from Birmingham Jail', King stressed upon the need for non-violent direct action, the inherent immorality and lack of justice in the existing laws and the probability that the African Americans might resort to bloodshed. "The Negro has many pent up resentments and latent frustrations, and he must release them. So let him march." The letter was an effort to bring the white politicians to the negotiating table before things turned violent.

King's letter was in response to the statement made by eight white clergymen from Alabama in 1963 where they accepted the existing social injustices but said that the battle should be fought in the courts and not on the streets. King differed in his view. He thought that without non-violent direct action, civil rights could never be achieved. "This wait has almost meant never."

The letter was King's attempt to draw the attention of the clergymen towards the pathetic living conditions of the blacks and how their silence about the unjust laws was contradicting the biblical tradition. King quoted greatly from **The Bible**. The letter was sensational and forced people to think of the toil of the blacks and aroused sympathy.

"I have a Dream"

In a seventeen minute public speech that went down in American history as one of the finest speeches, King asked for racial equality and an end to discrimination. Popularly referred to as "I have a Dream", the speech was delivered from the steps of the Lincoln Memorial during the March organized to protest against civil rights on Washington on August 28, 1963. The theme of the march was "jobs and freedom".

"Dr King had the power, the ability, and the capacity to transform those steps on the Lincoln Memorial into a monumental area that will forever be recognized. By speaking the way he did, he educated, he inspired, and he informed not just the people there, but people throughout America and unborn generations."(U.S. Representative John Lewis)

"I have a Dream"

America in the 1950's was far from the ideals of the equality of men as was stated in the Declaration of Independence. It was the time when there was discrimination against the Blacks, Hispanics and Asians.

Quoting from the Holy Bible and invoking the United States Declaration of Independence, the Emancipation Proclamation and the United States Constitution, the speech is universally hailed as a masterpiece of rhetoric. Quoting from Isaiah 40: 4-5, King said, "I have a dream that every valley shall be exalted". Drawing reference to the opening lines of Shakespeare's "Richard III", he remarked, "This sweltering summer of the Negro's legitimate discontent will not pass until there is an invigorating autumn..."

King Jr. at Lincoln Memorial

It is difficult to describe the fervor with which King spoke the text, carrying every heart along the emotional heights. The crowd not just listened but participated and could not stop applauding. It was definitely King's day as scores of Americans and Europeans listened on radio or watched on television the largest ever assemblage of people in America at the Lincoln Memorial.

The March on Washington put extreme pressure on the Kennedy administration to pass civil rights legislation in Congress. In the wake of his speech and march, the Time magazine named King Man of the Year for the year 1963. In 2004, the Library of Congress honored the speech by adding it to the United States National Recording Registry.

Immediately after the March, the civil rights leaders were asked by the New York Times Magazine to contribute to a symposium titled "What Next?" to which King responded "In a word—Now."He called for " immediate and effective Federal action to curb the shocking police brutality in the South," pointing out that the Justice Department was arresting blacks in Albany and Birmingham by making false statements.

Bloody Sunday

King, James Bevel, and the SCLC, in partial collaboration with SNCC, attempted to organize a march from Selma to the state capital of Montgomery, on March 7, 1965. The day came to be known as Bloody Sunday and was a major turning point in gaining public support for the Civil Rights Movement. The first attempt to organize the march remained unsuccessful due to violence against the demonstrators. King, however, remained absent from the march owing to his church duties. These set of three marches were organized asking for voting rights in the state of Alabama.

Montgomery Marches

By this time, white resistance to black voting rights had increased tremendously. As the tension between the two races was at an all time high, the organizing committee of the marches asked for King's help. The march organized on March 7, 1965 is remembered because the 600 peaceful protestors were brutally attacked by the state police.

Former Dallas County Sheriff Jim Clark, always wore a "Never" button on his uniform to show his opposition to the black voter registration was greatly instrumental in giving momentum to the Civil Rights Movement with his violent confrontations with marchers in Selma. He never regretted his actions.

After the police brutalities on March 7, when 600 civil rights marchers were attacked by state and local police with billy clubs and tear gas, the SCLC petitioned for injunction restraining order in the federal court against the State of Alabama. But the petition was denied and further organization of marches was also denied. Then, King himself organized a small march on March 9. However, the ended after King held a small prayer session at Edmund Pettus Bridge. He did this because he did not want to violate the court orders.

Violate to damage and destroy something; to go against a law

Civil rights leaders sought court protection for a third, full-scale march from Selma to the state capitol in Montgomery. The protection was duely provided to the protestors. So, on Sunday, March 21, about 3,200 marchers set out for Montgomery. They reached the capitol on March 25. By that time, the protestors were 25,000 in number. These protestors were adequately protected by 2,000 soldiers of the U.S. Army, 1,900 members of the Alabama National Guard, by FBI agents and Federal Marshals. It was five months later that the Voting Rights Act of 1965 was signed.

On the steps of the State Capitol, King delivered a speech known as "How Long Not Long".

"I have been to the mountain top"

King spoke on April 3, 1968, at the Mason Temple in Memphis, Tennessee, one day before his assassination. This last speech is known as "I Have Been to the Mountaintop" where he called for unified economic actions and non violent protests in the Memphis Sanitation Strike. His last speech is considered prophetic as King talked about the threats to his life.

Prophetic to say correctly about something that will happen in the future

The Assassination

It was in room 306 at the Lorraine Motel in Memphis where King was assassinated on April 4, 1968 at 39 years of age. King was shot at 6:01pm while standing on the second floor balcony of the motel's room. Immediately after he was shot, King was led to the hospital. He was, however, declared dead at 7:05 pm. King's last words before he died, he had uttered to musician Ben Branch who was to play at an event King was going to attend later that evening. He said, "Ben, make sure you play 'Take My Hand, Precious Lord' in the meeting tonight. Play it real pretty."

New York senator, Robert F. Kennedy, who was campaigning for the 1968 Democratic presidential nomination, was the first to announce King's assassination. His announcement was met with wailing and screams. Robert Kennedy urged the country to try and 'go beyond these rather difficult times' and unity between blacks and whites could make this happen.

To honour Dr King's deeply held beliefs, his colleagues called for non-violent means of protest against his assassination. Despite this call, America witnessed a nationwide wave of riots in more than 100 cities including Washington, Chicago and Baltimore. Dr King's funeral was attended by more than 300,000 people. The day was declared as the national day of mourning by President Johnson.

James Earl Ray, a fugitive from the Missouri State was accused of assassinating King. He was arrested at London's Heathrow Airport and was brought the US. He was sentenced to 99 years in prison. He finally died at 70 years of age in 1998.

The Nobel Peace Prize

Dr Martin Luther King, Jr. was awarded the Nobel Peace Prize in 1964 for his non-violent resistance to racial prejudice in America. He received the Noble Prize at 35 years of age, making him the youngest person to receive the honour. While accepting the prize, Dr King said that "every penny" of the prize money amounting to around $54,000 would be given to the Civil Rights Movement. The Prize honours acts "for the furtherance of brotherhood among men and to the abolishment or reduction

Prejudice an unaccountable dislike or preference towards a person, group or custom

of standing armies and for the extension of these purposes."

King Jr. was a terrific orator

In the Nobel Prize acceptance speech, Dr King stressed upon the prevailing situation in America where the black community was fighting against racial segregation. "I accept the Nobel Prize for Peace at a moment when twenty-two million Negroes of the United States of America are engaged in a creative battle to end the long night of racial injustice. I accept this award in behalf of a Civil Rights Movement which is moving with determination and a majestic scorn for risk and danger to establish a reign of freedom and a rule of justice.

Literary Contributions

Besides his speeches and papers which have been widely quoted, Martin Luther King. Jr. had also written many books. In addition to his autobiography, he also wrote **Strength to Love, The Measure of a man, Why We Can't Wait, A Testament of Hope, A Knock at Midnight, Where Do We Go from Here: Chaos or Community** and **Stride Toward Freedom: The Montgomery Story. A Testament of Hope** is a compilation of his famous sermons, public addresses and interviews.

King's heritage in the traditions of the southern black church is amply reflected in his writings. He had a sound knowledge of western philosophy and has used biblical theology to talk about various issues in his works.

The Legacy

There was a man who stood up for what he believed was right, who inspired others to do right, who fought injustice, who made a difference to the world - that was Martin Luther King, Jr., often considered among the few genuine prophets of the western world. He was a remarkable person who worked for humankind and towards the abolition of injustices. Unlike others, he went ahead and did everything possible to make his people break away from the shackles of racial discrimination. He advocated for universal brotherhood and equality. As a terrific orator, he reached out to the masses and again and again talked about equal rights for all. He was a man of not just his time but all times and all nations.